PIANO / VOCAL / GUITAR

# TWENTY ØNE PILØTS
## SCALED AND ICY

ISBN 978-1-70514-682-8

**HAL•LEONARD®**

Visit Hal Leonard Online at
**www.halleonard.com**

Contact us:
**Hal Leonard**
7777 West Bluemound Road
Milwaukee, WI 53213
Email: info@halleonard.com

In Europe, contact:
**Hal Leonard Europe Limited**
42 Wigmore Street
Marylebone, London, W1U 2RN
Email: info@halleonardeurope.com

In Australia, contact:
**Hal Leonard Australia Pty. Ltd.**
4 Lentara Court
Cheltenham, Victoria, 3192 Australia
Email: info@halleonard.com.au

T0050646

# CONTENTS

# GOOD DAY

Words and Music by
TYLER JOSEPH

I can feel my sat - u - ra - tion leav - ing me slow - ly.
Lost my job, my wife ___ and child, ___ ho - mie just sued me.

Broke the news on Mom's ___ va - ca - tion,
Shoot my life in shoot - 'em - up ___ style,

6

# SATURDAY

Words and Music by
TYLER JOSEPH

Moderate Dance groove

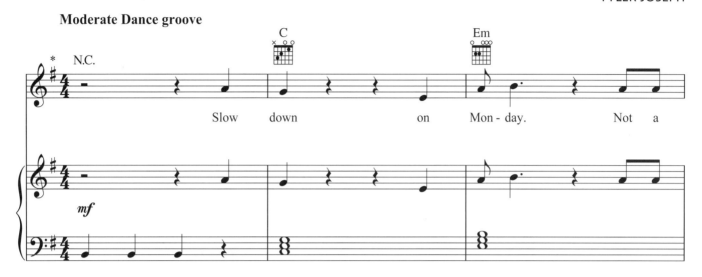

Slow down on Mon - day. Not a

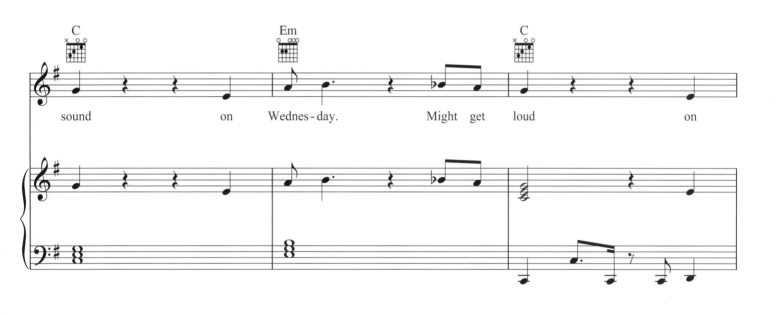

sound on Wednes - day. Might get loud on

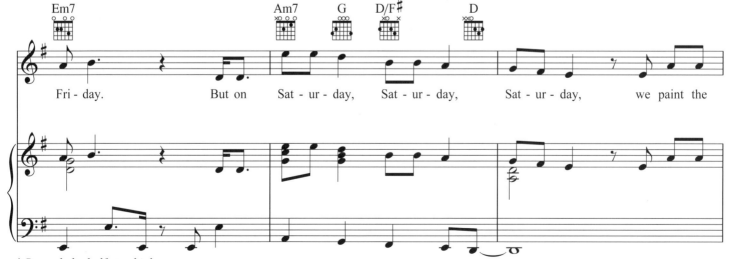

Fri - day. But on Sat - ur - day, Sat - ur - day, Sat - ur - day, we paint the

* *Recorded a half step higher.*

town. Lose my sense a time or two. ___ Weeks feel like days.

Med - i - cate ___ in the af - ter - noon. And I just ___ want to know: ___ have

you lost ___ your foot - ing, too? ___ I just pray that I'm not los - ing you.

Catch me float - ing cir - cles in my fish bowl. Keep things fresh. She said

# CHOKER

Words and Music by
TYLER JOSEPH

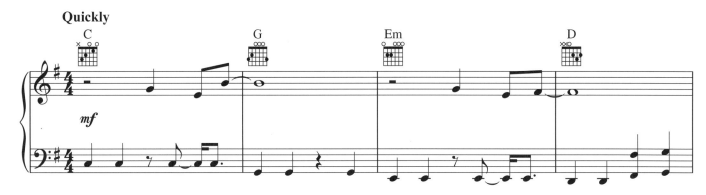

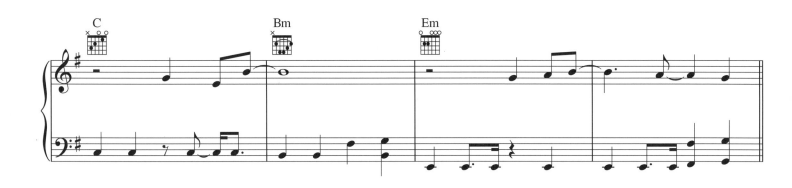

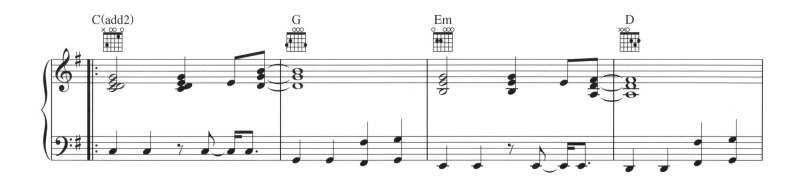

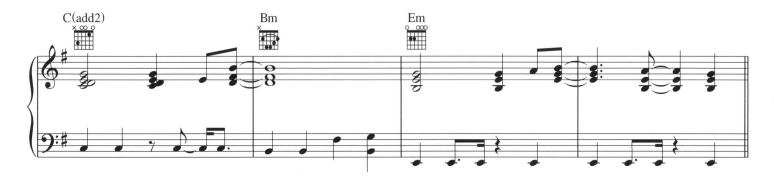

# SHY AWAY

Words and Music by
TYLER JOSEPH

**Bright Rock, in 2**

When I get __

__ home, __ you bet-ter not __ be there. __ We're plac - ing bets __

# THE OUTSIDE

Words and Music by
TYLER JOSEPH

**Moderate Pop**

am I on ___ the out - side?

Rap 2: *(see additional lyrics)*

*Additional Lyrics*

**Rap 1:** I am a Megalodon, ocean's feeling like a pond,
Swimming like a beast, underneath, they be clinging on.
Meteoric rise in prehistoric times
Now that meteor is coming, coming.
I am Megatron, cogs I'm stepping on.
Then the little cogs get together, start a renaissance.
Switch it up on me, for fuel efficiency
On fumes, I am running, running, running.

**Rap 2:** I'm on the outside
In the summer heat
You can pay the cover charge,
I'm in the street.
Little did they know
That they can't touch me.
I'm vibing, vibing.

# NEVER TAKE IT

Words and Music by
TYLER JOSEPH

**Moderately**

Ooh, ooh, ___ ooh, ooh, ___ ooh, ooh, ___

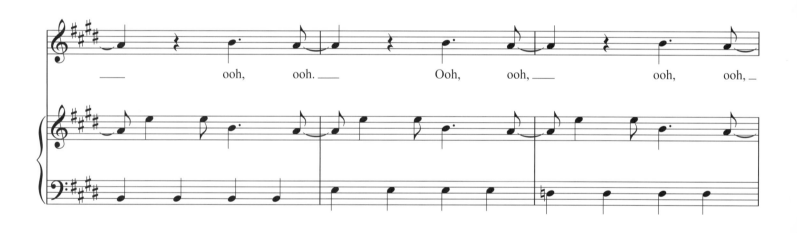

___ ooh, ooh. ___ Ooh, ooh, ___ ooh, ooh, ___

___ ooh, ooh, ___ ooh. Now __ that they know ___
Why __ cure dis - ease ___

To Coda

they're ask-in' for a sec-ond try. You and I, ___ we'll nev-er take it.

Ooh, ooh, ___ ooh, ooh, ___ ooh, ooh, ___

___ ooh, ooh, ___ ooh, ooh, ___ ooh.

Ooh, ooh, ___ ooh, ooh, ___ ooh, ooh, ___

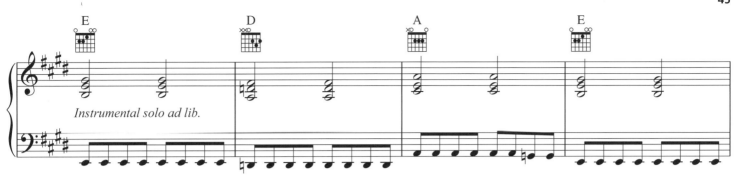

*Instrumental solo ad lib.*

**D.S. al Coda**

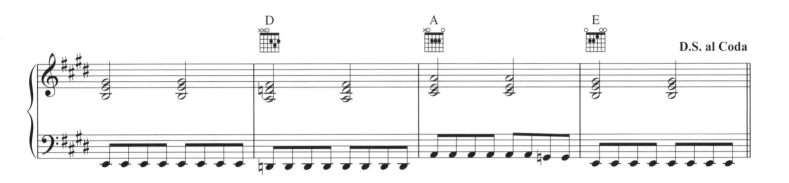

**CODA**

Ooh, ooh, ___ ooh, ooh, ___ ooh, ooh, ___ ooh, ooh. ___

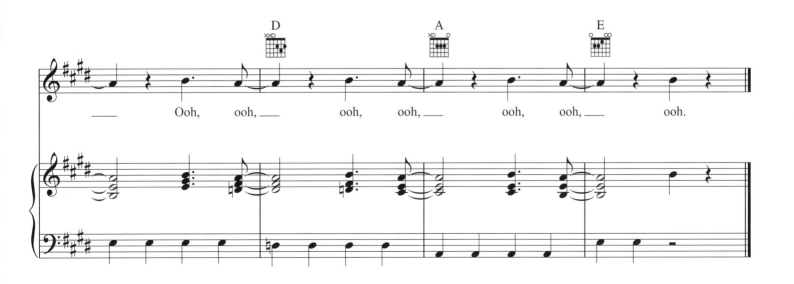

___ Ooh, ooh, ___ ooh, ooh, ___ ooh, ooh, ___ ooh.

# MULBERRY STREET

Words and Music by
TYLER JOSEPH

# FORMIDABLE

Words and Music by
TYLER JOSEPH

**Pop Rock**

Lyrics:

You __ are for-mid-a-ble to __ me 'cause you __ seem to

know it, where you want to go. Yeah, __ yeah, yeah, I'll fol - low you.

# REDECORATE

Words and Music by
TYLER JOSEPH

**Half-time Urban feel**

*\* Recorded a half-step lower.*

*Additional Lyrics*

**Rap:** With the bells and the whistles scaled back
Like an isolated track.
And he feels trapped when he's not inebriated,
Fair to say he's fairly sedated most days of the week.
He might have made it if he lived on a different street.
I repeat, scaled back and isolated.
He says he likes an open schedule, but he mostly hates it.
If you're running to his room, take a breath before you break in.
Put your ear up to the door, tell me, can you hear him saying?

# BOUNCE MAN

Words and Music by
TYLER JOSEPH

**Upbeat, with a lilt**

You should bounce, bounce, bounce, man, come to the house, man,

I'll let my old ___ la-dy know. ___ You'll be in and out, out, out, man.

Float you a cou-ple bands, then you head to Mex-i-co. ___

bounce, bounce, bounce, man, come to the house, man. We'll sing one ___ more song, ___

___ so long. ___

I'll let my old ___ la - dy know, ___ so long. ___

Then you head to Mex - i - co. ___

G           Bm/F♯         Am

She's been cry - ing, but I'll tell her you're fine. ___ Don't mat - ter now, ___

D.S. al Coda

D           D/E   D/F♯

___ if you ___ need a piece, ___ I'll break ___ it down. ___ You should

CODA         C          G

___ so long. ___ Da da da, ba da da da. ___

Em           D          C

I'll let my old ___ la - dy know, ___ so long. ___ Da da da,

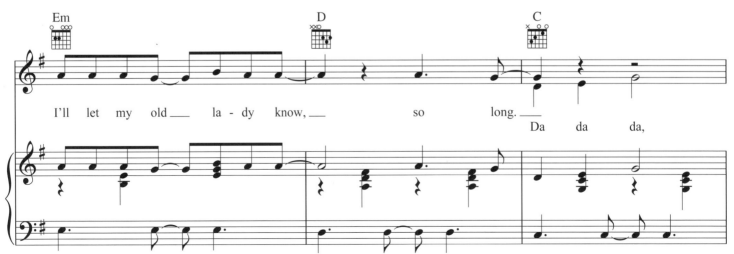

# NO CHANCES

Words and Music by
TYLER JOSEPH

*Additional Lyrics*

**Rap 1:** In my house, shoes in a foot race. In this house we got feng shui.
Get the door to blow you away. Flamethrower, you a switchblade.
Feet planted on grip tape with my shoulders squared and my back straight.
Got a good base and a loose tongue. Notorious in the octagon, now.

**Rap 2:** How'd you get the location, put together pieces?
They say they sell the information in those terms of agreement.
We spend some weekends on the grind, surveillance is outside.
We see when you arrive, ride or die my son.
Spent some weekends on the grind, surveillance is outside.
We see when you arrive, ride or die my son.